WHAT IS YOUR CORE BUSINESS?

A paradigm shift for suicide prevention.

How parents, teachers and the community can help teenagers achieve maturity safely and happily without mental distress.

S R Cheyne

Book design and production:
diypublishing.co.nz

BRS Publishing

shelleycheyne@gmail.com

ISBN 978-0-473-49526-8

A catalogue record for this book is available from the
National Library of New Zealand

To Vikki, for helping me find my boat lift.

Contents

Foreword

It was the Fourth of July, my birthday. On my way to work, after dropping my son off at school, there were traffic delays. An 18-year-old boy had been hit by a train. I later found out that in the previous year 668 people had taken their own lives in New Zealand. This was heart–breaking.

Suicide is a subject seldom discussed. Media reports suggest that more and more people, from celebrities to Joe Average on the corner, are seeing taking their own life as an option. All too often they are young, still on the threshold of life. It is a tragic fact and something has got to be done about it.

When the topic is discussed, a common theme, repeatedly heard, is, *If you think someone is at risk support them and reach for the appropriate services as soon as possible.* This is an ambulance at the bottom of the cliff approach. I want to catch people while they are still at the top of the cliff, fence off the risk before any drama ensues.

If, by writing this book, I can change the mindset of just one person, it will have served its purpose. It is not intended as a means to analyse why young people have tragically taken their lives, to try to solve the mystery of *WHY?* If your teenager is in the midst of severe anxiety and/or depression, this book is not what you're looking for. There may be ideas that will resonate, but those already at risk should seek immediate medical help or intervention.

I have worked in healthcare over the past 23 years, and the ideas in this book are based largely upon what I have seen in my practice, augmented by personal reading and study. I am a parent, so also reflected are conversations I have had with my children. I believe that the ideas I have developed can help people to function and have a purpose and to find their true, authentic self: that is, a whole person with a healthy life, good nutrition, good work–life balance and a robust mental state.

This book proposes a shift in thinking. It prompts you to ask personal questions to target the mindset that, in the young, engenders depression and anxiety, so that suicide is no longer considered to be an option.

I concede that some people will read this book and hate it, as it is seriously confronting in nature. If that is your response, however, please pause and ask yourself why?

Introduction

Before I go any further let me emphasise that this book does not ask you to stop observing basic laws, rules or value systems. If you are of school age you still have to go to school. If you are working, you still need to go to work. In today's society there are certain basic expectations that have to be lived and abided by.

In order to be truly happy, people need to have a solid understanding of their identity. By understanding their identity and accepting it, people know where and how they fit into their community and society. Establishing what I have called your *core business* helps to define your identity. It helps you to define and create a social structure that works for the real you, enables you to be your real self.

As teenagers come of age they have to decide on their future pathways. To make a fully informed decision, they need to question themselves honestly on what they want, and how they will achieve it? A parent's task is to guide her child openly and honestly towards *his*[1] goals and not towards what they think is best for them.

Many of the ideas in this book diverge from traditional cultural thinking. It advocates having open conversations about your personal core business, as a child and as a parent. It is easy to know what is right for your family. What is right for the individual child, however, may be quite different from what the family and society have done in the past. This does not mean that an alternative viewpoint is wrong. Core business is about discovering and considering an approach to life that supersedes what you have discovered and considered in the past. If you live a fruitful life, in good health and well being—conventional or not—then you have achieved happiness.

For many people these ideas will seem like simple common sense. They deal with issues that people are confronted with daily, and with natural process that leads to a solution that does not engender anxiety or depression or suicide.

---

1   In the interests of gender equality, 'he/she', 'him/her' and 'his/hers' are represented randomly by the male and female pronouns.

Regard these ideas, therefore, as a checklist or guide that show you are on the right track.

I believe strongly that, if the basic concepts are followed mindfully, people will find their true path.

The Core Business Of a Child
is To Be Awesome

Most of this book concerns teenagers coming of age and making decisions that will affect their future.

In order to become a teenager, people have to go through the beginning steps of being a child. It is here where they are introduced to the activities that develop them into multifaceted individuals. They go to school to develop their brain. They undertake responsibilities in the household, such as chores. They participate in different hobbies and sports. And they play. Some activities they may like and some they may not. There are some things they must do and some which they may drop at the end of a term or a school year. Some pursuits cultivate their imagination and others that simply allow them to be and to have fun. There are elements that are structured and elements that are non-structured. All of them add to the toolbox of things they can do.

By playing, children learn to entertain themselves. They develop their imagination and they learn to get along with others in a non-structured way. When they play they begin to get an idea of things they like, which they can develop later. Good parents introduce new things to try, no pressure, just fun. Hobbies, sports and dancing, for example, help to develop perseverance and process. They provide a framework that help make children well–rounded as they enter their teenage years.

A child's core business is quite basic and can be broken down into:

1. Waking up and getting dressed [either on their own or with help].

2. Eating breakfast, lunch, dinner and any snacks in between, as well as drinking water and other fluids.

3. Going to school, whether mainstream, home schooled or specialised.

4. Doing jobs around the house.

5. Playing, either by themselves or with others.

6. Observing basic hygiene.

7. Going to bed and sleeping at a reasonable time.

Parents define the core business of a child, and guide them through their basic responsibilities. Some children take on too much at a young age, depending on their birth order or just their personalities in general. They take on responsibility for the core business of others (eg, siblings or classmates), but not attending to their own core business can impact their health. It may lead to feelings of frustration and anxiety, for, no matter what they do, they have no control over other people's actions. As parents, by taking responsibility for guiding our children through the core business of being a child, we are allowing them to be children. Everything else is the responsibility of the adults, and not that of a child.

The children of today are more knowing than those of previous generations and often appear to be older than they are. They can even articulate in ways that appear mature, but they are still only as old as their chronological age. As parents we should not be misled by this, and should consistently promote our children's core business to them. This does not mean that we wrap them in cotton wool so that they are oblivious to everything going on around them. This is what gives them a depth of character and understanding of the real world. We can have honest conversations and show them raw emotion at an age–appropriate level, but remind them of what is the core business of a child, and how anything else is not yet for them.

We want our children to be great adults. We want them to strive to be the most awesome version of themselves that they possibly can be. This will give them confidence to grow and learn, ready to step up as they approach the teenage years.

What Is Your Core Business?

Have you ever been in a situation where you are doing something because you think you should? It is not necessarily what you want to do, but you know it will make your parents or your friends or your teachers etc happy?

There comes a time when the objects or activities or jobs we choose need to be something that we are truly passionate about. That is our *Core Business*. It defines who we are and what we need to be. The crazy thing about this is that we do not need to follow a single direction. We can have interests in all kinds of areas. What we choose could include total polar opposites, and guess what? That is OK!

So how do we identify our core business? It is a little voice deep within us[2].If we listen carefully it keeps us on the straight and narrow. The hard part is to listen to that voice, for often it may diverge from what you have always thought right for you. If it is not properly managed it will engender anxiety and fear. If it is managed successfully, we can trustfully undertake a myriad of activities without fear, when managed life is easy.

Teenagers will find discovering their core business a challenge, which may be real or perceived. The support of a parent, trusted adult or friend is often required. Some of the key challenges are as follows.

1] *"If I like this [whatever thing] what if my friends think I'm weird and won't like me."*

A wise adult might advise that it is okay to tell your friends that you like this [whatever thing], that you own that statement and are confident in your decision, so why would your friends not like you? You are not responsible for what your friends think just as they are not responsible for deciding what you think. If you are empowered by your own choices there is no drama. You like it, you don't care what they think. Or: you do care, but it is a simple case of agreeing to disagree. Their thoughts should not influence your

---

2   The inner voice referred to is basic subconscious thought in the absence of schizophrenia or other complex personality disorders.

decision one way or the other. If they do not accept what you like, maybe you are in the wrong friend group and need to find another.

Chances are that what you like, they might secretly like as well, but are too timid to say so for fear of being mocked.

There is always something that draws friends together. Having interests in common is definitely a good start, but ultimately it comes down to shared value systems. Trust yourself to base your friendships are based on you, the person, not what you do. Let your friends get to know the real you.

2] *"What if I want to do this [whatever career path], and it is not what my parents have planned for me. They will be so disappointed"*

Choosing a career path is a very daunting time for many teenagers. It can cause a lot of angst. The number one worry is, *what if I get it wrong?* It is particularly difficult where a family business has been passed down for generations.

The answer is very simple. *There is no wrong!* Follow your heart, do something you are passionate about. Something, that, when the alarm goes off in the morning, you cannot wait to get up. Something that if you won the Lotto, you would still go to work every day. When you do something you love then it is fun, no matter how hard you must work, and it brings you absolute joy and happiness. Of course, you should also be able to make ends meet, pay your bills and have a lifestyle that suits you. Different occupations have different pay scales. But if you do something you love for the right reasons, you will have a wealth that you cannot quantify.

You have to tell your parents in all honesty that the family business does not define your own core business. You have to explain why this is not for you. It is up to your parents to listen. They may be disappointed, but their task is to support and guide you on your core business, with outcomes that are best for you.

If you choose a particular career path and, as you are studying or working, you realise that it is not for you, you have not *failed*. If you interpret 'fail' as 'First Attempt In Learning'[3] you can change to an occupation that better suits you. The decision is yours, part of your core business, of what you want to do with your life.

By owning your core business there is no drama, you gain self worth and you define who you are as a person. If you are challenged you can confidently state, *Well I like it, end of story.*

---

3   *FAIL: first attempt in Learning*, A.P.J. Abdul Kalam, Quoteistan.com

3] *"I am feeling overwhelmed by life?"*

In a teenager's world there can be many things happening, some real and some perceived. There can be personal issues: school work, puberty, activities, relationships, clothes, what the future holds, social media status—or it can be things happening around them— parents' divorce, sibling in trouble, financial problems. A major anxiety with teenagers is the fear that people are judging them—which may or may not be true.

The important issue is how teenagers perceive this pressure, and how they keep a solid perspective. By being able to identify what is core business in this scenario, they decrease the feeling of being overwhelmed. They are able to focus their energy where it should be focussed and to see how little there is to be concerned about. They realise that they are not responsible for other people's actions and feelings. A teenager's natural reaction, however, is to shut down and process these thoughts themselves. This can be challenging, as they may not completely understand what it is that is overwhelming them. At such times, they need to have a conversation with a parent, trusted adult or a friend who can remind them that these thoughts are normal, to stay aligned to their core business, and to trust that, in the end, all will be well.

Of course, they do care what other people think, and that is fine as long as they don't let it prevent them from maintaining their true path. They cannot, in any case, control or change how other people think. Accepting that stops the backchat in their heads and focusses them on what is going on. Without being mean or rude, they are able to keep themselves safe at all times. With love and support from people in there lives, all will be well.

Big Girl Knickers/Big Boy Pants

It is hard for a teen to take a stance on an issue without knowing what his peers will think. *Will they judge me? Will they like me?*

In the real world it's OK to have your own opinions or to do things differently. It is OK to like things different from those your peers like. The hard part is to own the difference. Friends may tease or hassle, but this where you learn *grit*. You accept that your ideas are different and soldier on.

Sometimes, when friends are managing their own core business, one friend may not want to be part of the relationship anymore. It is not personal, and definitely not about you. Your friend is not neglecting you but simply doing what is best for her core business. If you can accept this, then you can focus on your own core business. Put on your big girl knickers/big boy pants[4] and focus on what is most important for you. The hurt may still be there, but you will understand what is going on.

This may also happen in loving relationships. It is important for both parties to attend to their own core business. Being in a relationship sits high in many people's priorities, to the point where it defines self, rather than simply being part of core business. By maintaining your own integrity, you maintain the integrity of the relationship. You are not defined by it, you are defined by who you are. In a sound relationship both parties always respect one another, and do what they can to help their partner be the best that they can be.

Putting on your big girl knickers or big boy pants becomes necessary if the relationship breaks up or if one partner is not treating the other with respect [eg, being a bit controlling]. It can be a devastating time, but it is important to remember what actually defines who you are, the person knowing and pursuing your core business. If the relationship is not working it is best ended in mutual respect and friendship.

---

4   *Time to Put on your Big Girl Knickers/Big Boy Pants*, DNC Chair Debbie Wasserman Schulz.

This is the time, when a friend is suddenly not a friend anymore, or if a relationship has broken up, that a teen needs to *have a conversation*. It doesn't matter who with, but she needs to have one with. You may be a parent, another adult or a trusted friend. Your role is to remind her about the importance of *core business*. You can give her some honest perspective, whether the issue is playground (or cyber) bullying, fractured friendships or a broken relationship. You will let her know if she is overreacting, or that something needs further attention. Between the two of you, you can come up with a solution.

When a young person takes his life, the common reaction is, *Why didn't he talk to someone? Why wasn't there a conversation?* The problem is that it was already too late. People in the depths of depression or anxiety lack the capacity to judge whether their situation is perceived or real. At this point it is too late to talk about it.

If she had a conversation with a supportive parent or friend at the time she were starting to express her doubts and fears, she could have refocussed on her *core business*, and the problem shared would have become the problem halved.

Success In Sport

If you are involved in a sport, you should get from it an undying love or joy. When you participate, you love the pain you feel as you push yourself up to and beyond your usual limits, and the absolute desire to win, to be the best athlete that you possibly can be.

In the early days, say from three to twelve years old, children should experience a wide range of sports, to develop skills and resilience, to determine what kind of activities they like. Some kids love sports from the beginning and some do not, but learning to exercise individually or in a team is good for both mind and body.

The sport in which people choose to participate, always comes down to individual preference. They may be very good at sport, training hard and, when competing, doing well. They may win and they may not. Though they want to win, and have trained hard, so have all the other participants in their chosen activity.

All players can do on the day is trust that their training programme is effective, trust their ability and go hard. Everyone competing on the day wants that. If they don't win after giving it their all, sadly that is just where they are at. Playing better next time is the all-important lesson. Grit is again valuable—to get up, train hard and do all they can to improve for next time. If an athlete has that true passion to compete and win they will do this easily.

Parents and coaches must be realistic here too, for the individual and the team. There will be no added value in just screaming at the athletes. Their skill and stamina are where they are at on the day. Remembering this point gives sport a true perspective. It is a game, especially at the under– twenty level, though that is not always appreciated by the players. The teenage brain can perceive loss as the worst thing in the world, which in turn can set up conditions for further anxiety and depression. As adults we need to acknowledge loss, even be gutted on behalf of the team, but what we articulate to our kids is that we will do better next time, and in reflection to learn the lesson.

If a keen sports player finds joy in the sport but also loves schoolwork or the job or some other activity—what then? They still have the opportunity to compete, but must be realistic in their commitment to training, social occasions and actual competition. They can still enjoy the sport and not resent it.

With sport, as with other activities, your core business comes down to what you want to achieve, and how much time and effort you can dedicate to it. You have to acknowledge that you can't always win. If you do, great! If you beat your previous target, great! If you finish, great! If you break it down to that, and recognise that you have done all you can do, the pressure to win at all costs is immediately removed. The joy of the sport is restored.

All this works better if parents and coaches are supporting young players in a positive way, aware that they are only as good as the competition on the day, and tailoring their criticism accordingly.

Being good at sport and loving it are not the same thing. Some athletes may be very good at what they do, but it might not be their passion. This is a difficult dilemma, for promise in a sport can bring great opportunity, but it will not necessarily bring happiness.

At the end of the day the sport has to be something the athlete wants to do for themselves and not to be a vehicle for their parents' dream. If the sport does not truly belong in the player's core business, he or she must be able to say so safely and to participate in the sport they prefer.

This is where those honest conversations with parents and peers are valuable, establishing the right to be respected and valued for taking ownership of her core business. If the player is challenged or teased for not having a love for the sport, this will engender the confidence to counter any such bullying.

The hardest part of being a teenager is understanding what is going on, and the fear of what people will think. If young players can articulate that they do *not* want to participate in a sport at a particular level and know that they are permitted to do this, they will realise that this is legitimate personal choice, and not the worst thing in the world that could possibly happen.

Success at School

Going to school can be a very productive time for students, as there are so many basic life skills to be learned. School is not only for academic achievement, but for determining who you are as a person; what you like and dislike; how you get along with your peers; and developing the confidence to be yourself.

There are two clear categories of students—those who love school and those who don't. Both can present their own challenges. If students understand this, and have the backing of regular conversations with a support person [ie, a trusted adult, a parent or a friend], going to school can be what it is meant to be, a definitive learning experience.

The students who love to go to school have a drive for academic achievement. Where success can provide opportunity not only in terms of school qualifications, but also as a foundation for further tertiary study and scholarships. This can put tremendous pressure on students to perform.

Secondary school is designed to make students jump through hoops. If they go to school, are present in class and do their homework, nine out of ten will pass their exams and obtain their high school/college qualification. At its best the system is designed to teach kids to focus, prioritize, practice time management and figure out what their core business is.

The problem that arises from this system is not with students who are struggling academically, but with the very high achievers who put an unrealistic amount of pressure on themselves. Often they are already involved in several extra-curricular activities, maybe also have a part–time job, and want to achieve the highest-grade levels as well. With the amount of work they are putting in that they are achieving at a very high level, and will probably do well in their external exams and internal assessments. However, they do not believe it. They can make themselves ill by striving to get the perfect grade.

This is where they need help to define their core business for school. They need to be present, to complete their work and pass their tests to get through the hoops. They need to accept that the work they have done will give them an adequate grade. And if they have any doubts at all they should have a conversation.

Then there are the students who hate school. They may be bright enough to achieve at a high level, but academic pursuits are not part of their core business. The challenge that these students face is identifying what their core business is. If they know that they hate school, that is fine, but what do they love? What would they like to pursue further? This is hard for many students as they need to have a very honest conversation with themselves, followed by an honest conversation with their parents. In this instance, school is a stepping stone to their career. They still need to get through the hoops, but when they have direction it will be easier.

Many parents have had an idea in their head of what will be the best path for their children. It may be following in the family business or getting further education that the parents did not achieve. It may be a career based solely on financial gain. However great the parents' intentions for their children, it is not the children's path, and it is not for parents to determine the core business of their child. Their role is to advise, suggest, perhaps play devil's advocate, but ultimately support their children to determine their true core business. Parents must reassure them that it is OK to change their mind if their original choice was not in fact right for them. It's OK to sit down and reassess, find better choices. Remember, treading a new path is not a FAIL, just a *first attempt in learning*.

When students who hate school are supported and encouraged to engage in their true core business, they will be successful. They will be passionate about what they want to do, and have the drive to follow through. They will probably be better members of society, because they are pursuing their core business, and they are less likely to get into trouble. Their mental state will also be better, as they are supported in doing something they place value on. This is ultimately what we want for our children, for them to be happy and secure in doing something they love. We need to remind them that their peers may disagree or make fun of them but they are OK if they own their core business and have support when they need it.

Arts and Culture

The world we live in is multicultural and it is important to respect and appreciate the different cultures that surround us, including our own. Having a cultural identity paves the way to your core business, for it pervades all that we do.

Teens need to know that it is OK to incorporate your culture into your daily life. Your culture is part of what defines you as a person, and it is healthy to take complete ownership of that. This may mean that your family's beliefs and customs are different from those of your friends. You may have ritual activities that you practice, because they align with the beliefs and value systems of your culture. It may mean that the food you eat is different to what your friends eat. This does not mean what you eat is wrong—it is just different, is all. As long as what you eat fulfills your daily requirement as a teenager, it really doesn't matter.

Some people do not understand other cultures, and because it is different to their own. They may ridicule others' beliefs and practices and appear cruel or mean. As we all know this is ethically unacceptable, but unfortunately it is something that happens. Your culture is not a secret to be hoarded. It is something that helps define you, and it is up to you to let people know that—*It is who I am and that's how it is.*

Sometimes lines may be blurred and people want to mix their culture. Is this right or is this wrong? It is a way to have an open conversation while affirming the core business of each individual. Respect for your culture must be maintained, but so must respect to yourself. Many communities are made up of a melting pot of differing cultures, so what was traditionally valid may have changed. If you break it down, difference is OK. If your teen is a good member of society, treats people well and respects your culture, then a conversation about changing boundaries within a culture can take place. This open communication decreases the potential for anxiety or depression, and reduces the enticement of suicide. Conversely, it may promote happiness, as the individual takes ownership of core business.

Cultural activities have value and need to be allocated time and energy. They maintain traditions, teach the history of families and communities, and give the participant a better sense of personal identity.

The Arts falls into a similar category. People participating in a choir, a theatre production, or dance, for example, strive to perform to the absolute best of their ability. As with sports, children 3–12 years old should be introduced to a variety of arts to develop their artistic talents, and to help identify which discipline they want to pursue further. Some children love the experience, and some tolerate it because their parents believe it is important. In either case, the brain development that can take place in these years is valuable in the growth of the child.

As the years progress, further development becomes a matter of individual choice. Participants must expect to train hard, and to make sacrifices to perform at their best. There must be willing to push, to take criticism, and to reflect and push again. They must keep their perspective, especially when performing at a competition or examination. As with sport, so with the arts, which can be performed for the love of it or at a more social level requiring not so much dedication to it. It is important to set boundaries appropriately.

Performance art can be a group activity, where the challenge for the participant is collaboration and teamwork. Learning to take personal responsibility is paramount for the teenager, especially in group situations. All performing artists can do is prepare themselves, do the best they can and trust that the rest of their team have done the same. In a team setting, individual performers have absolutely no control over what the rest of the team is doing. They can try to encourage and persuade, but they cannot do the work that their teammate is responsible for. There is no point, therefore, in worrying about whether or not their teammates will do their part. Their control extends only to themselves and that is all. That is why teamwork can be difficult, as everyone has to pull together, all have to do their part and to trust their teammates will do the same. When, on the day, the performance comes together, the core business is achieved.

Parents, Know Your Role

If you want your kids to grow into capable, independent adults, give them space to make some decisions without you controlling their every move.

Back off! Let them try. Let them fail.

It's not about them always getting it right, it's learning not to be afraid to try.

Brooke Hampton.

Being a parent is probably one of the hardest jobs you will ever undertake. You have brought a child into this world who is a combination of two entirely separate individuals, who may share particular value systems or may have an entirely different agenda.

A parent's role is to be an absolute support system, whose many components nurture the growth of a beautiful adult. Some parental tasks are quite straightforward, common sense if you will. They include feeding children, making sure they get enough sleep, allowing them to relax, getting them from here to there. More important are helping them to determine their core business (even where it does not align with expectations) by being present when needed, showing unconditional love by constructive questioning and discussion and by wise guidance and advice.

The body is a very intricate biochemical system, which if properly fed and nurtured can operate at a highly effective rate. A teen's nutritional needs are a whole lot greater than an adult's. Their vitamin and mineral requirements are almost doubled to those of an adult[5]. This is hugely important for, if these requirements are not met, the teenage body cannot function to its optimum potential. The main reason for this is all the growth and development happening within the teenage body. As a parent you need to constantly observe, question and support to ensure your child is getting his essential nutrients.

---

5   *Stay Healthy By Supplying what is Lacking in your Diet*, researched by David Coory.

The problem is that many teenagers cannot be bothered to eat and do not place any importance on healthy food. Therefore, proper nutrition has to be made a part of your family's basic routine. If anyone complains, it falls into *this is just how it is* category.

Teenage nutrition must always be related to child's core business, especially when it involves sports training, performance rehearsals, recreational activities requiring high levels of energy and endurance—although even for day-to-day living, nutrition has to be considered. Teens need three solid meals a day: breakfast, lunch and dinner, with snacks available in between. Regular meal times reinforce the this is how it is principle.

Eating regularly will fuel a teen's chemistry, supporting high level of performance, and an even mental state chemically based on serotonin that induces calm and melatonin that promotes healthy sleep. The calmness is important, as it buttresses a realistic perspective. When an event is pending or school work is due the teen will approach it with a tranquil mind, knowing that things will be OK.

Ensuring that your teenager also gets adequate iron is paramount. It is iron and the absorption of iron, which helps to decrease fearfulness in teenagers, to maintain attention span, and to provide growth and energy to muscles and the body[6].

Teenagers need to get adequate sleep, and good sleep is based on basic chemistry once again. Eating at regular times throughout the day helps to produce melatonin, a neurotransmitter that enables sleep. It is produced by having protein at breakfast and lunch, and something sweet four hours after waking and again four hours after that. This would equate to a morning and afternoon snack, which would produce insulin in the body. This would convert the protein from breakfast and lunch to glucagon, which passes through the blood brain barrier to produce serotonin, then melatonin[7]. If both of these neurotransmitters are present, resulting in calm and sleep, it is highly unlikely that a person will suffer from anxiety or depression.

As a parent, you can promote the importance of sleep to your teenager, and get him to go to bed and get up at a reasonable time, and in doing so wake up feeling rested. If this is not happening, you need to have a conversation.

Correct mindful breathing gently fills the lungs with oxygen while inflating the abdominal cavity. It is relaxes the shoulders, the mind and stimulates the prefrontal cortex of the brain[8] reducing the likelihood of anxiety or depression.

6 *Stay Healthy By Supplying what is Lacking in your Diet,* researched by David Coory.

7 *Balance Your Body's Chemistry and Feel Uplifted,* Matt Church

8 *The Reality Check,* Heidi Haavik

Confirm your children are breathing correctly.

The teenage body grows and changes rapidly physically, neurologically and mentally. Throughout the growth period it is not uncommon for injury to occur, that can interrupt the pattern of growth laid out by the body. If your child gets hurt make sure that they receive the appropriate treatment to assist their healing—for example, physiotherapy, chiropractic, osteopathy or massage. These therapies help to realign the body's structure, so that the growth process can be accelerated. Teenagers have enough to focus on without complicating things by healing incorrectly.

Children need the opportunity to have down time. They need to learn how to relax in a non-structured way, either by themselves or with others. It is at this time, they can learn to really laugh. They can learn that is OK to be silly, and if people are laughing with you or at you, it is not a personal attack but just fun. This is when memories are made and depth of self is discovered. If your children are following their own core business, then they will be hanging out with like-minded people, rather than people who make them feel bad. The boundaries of play are set by the children/teenagers and if left to it can have a lot of fun.

Life in the 21st century is very fast paced. Many families have both parents working, or are single parent households with one parent working. Each day brings the constant logistics of getting everyone to where they have to be at the right time.

Most families nowadays have multiple electronic devices. Technology is fun and a great way to keep people quiet, focused and not causing trouble, but it has to be used respectfully and with boundaries.

Teenagers need their parents to be present. They need to be able to talk to them and ask questions. Parents in turn need to see their teens' expressions and body language and to assess where they're at. Often teenagers will say that everything is OK, but if their behaviour is off, it is a parent's job to probe, to gauge their mood or even just the look in their eyes, to monitor their eating and sleeping patterns, to consider whether they could be using drugs or alcohol. This is where a parent can help and guide them, remind them of their core business. If teenagers feel that they have the unconditional support of their parents, it will help them to remain calm and feel happy.

Parents know what they would like their children to be and to achieve. They want them to be successful, healthy and happy. They know and understand that there are things their children need to do to achieve such happiness. The challenge is that children often have a different interpretation of what success and happiness means. They may share their parents' ambitions or go in a different direction altogether. The important thing for parents to remember is that their job is to guide, not direct.

Parenting isn't just about career choices, of course. The teenage years are about discovery, about learning their sexuality, about their spiritual choices and about where they fit into the world. Parents teach their children values that fit into their own belief systems. It is important however to acknowledge that, although traditional values are cherished, the world is different to what it once was. It is OK for a family member to not conform to the traditional ways. She or he might be lesbian, gay, bisexual or transgender, or just follow a different religious faith. The one thing that will never change is that they will always be their parents' children and rely on them for support and guidance.

The challenge for parents is that their teen's choices may not align with the family's values, and it may be a real struggle to accept the choices that she has made. The fear of judgmental criticism from their community is a reality, and that can be hard. However, as a parent you need to ask yourself 'Am I a good mum or dad?' 'Is my child a good person?' 'Is my child kind and supportive of her loved ones? Does she strive to be the best she can be in a way respectful of others?' If the answer is 'Yes', then you have a good parent who has raised a good child uninfluenced by others' beliefs and priorities.

Children want their parent's approval. They will go down a particular path—even if for them it is not core business—to make their parents happy. This may involve activities at which they are very talented and can manage it with ease. However, if it is not really part of their core business they will never be truly happy.

If a child is brought up to do exactly what she is told without question, she will never go against her parents. However, she is not engaging with her core business, so will not be happy.

Many parents encourage their children to strive for absolute perfection. As most want to please their parents, striving towards this goal creates a constant pressure to perform flawlessly in whatever they undertake. The work they present is never good enough. Without a perfect score even the best result is a failure. Children cannot function, mentally or physically, at this level of intensity. This will put massive pressure on those prone to anxiety and depression. It is something they may not grow out of, that will colour their whole lives.

Does this mean that in supporting your children and helping them to determine their core business, you relinquish all parental responsibility? Because their path is not our own, it is easy to feel that we are letting our children down, and not helping them be as successful as we would wish. We need to reflect that it is not about us. Their idea of success may be, and perhaps should be, totally different to ours, but successful all the same. If we deny our children our support in finding their core business, there will be battles, and being a parent will not seem like a good option.

Don't give up on your children. You need to question and probe to determine if their children have properly identified and are managing their core business—if their behaviour is off, probe even more. But step back and check that they have room to grow in their own unique way.

This can be difficult, because, if your child's path has a direction you do not like, or are even embarrassed about, do you interfere? Let your child articulate to you why this path is important to him, and please listen. His preferences may be explained in a way that you had not considered and discovered before. It is OK to give an opinion or the other side of the story, but at the end of the day, only the individual can decide, *What is my core business?*

Why Am I Different? Am I OK?

As puberty starts in the early teenage years there are many changes happening within the body at a physical and emotional level. It is not unusual for teenagers to have a heightened sense of anxiety during this change, but they have no real explanation for it. They are very self conscious about the changes in their bodies, not just at a physical level about themselves, but about everything that is happening to and around them. They do not under any circumstances want to be the centre of attention.

Their perspective is that anything happening in their life could potentially bring about social disaster and that people would most certainly judge or ridicule them. Of course, this is not true, but to a teenager it is all–important. The sad truth is often that things, good and bad, happen and that is just how it is, so all a teenager can really do is just accept it and move on.

It could be a physical change, which of course puberty always entails. A teenager may grow taller, get bigger, have pimples, be hairy, develop breasts or change voice pitch. These are natural physical changes, not something to be ashamed about or to hide from. It is what it is. If anyone else feels that there is place to comment on a teenager's physical changes that he does not have any control over, there is no point to his getting upset about it. It is probably not even personal—sometimes people make others feel bad because they feel bad about themselves.

All teenagers can do is acknowledge and move on, remembering not to be mean in the process. They can say, *I'm doing my best here, please support me*. They can make a positive statement, accepting the change: *I am tall and I am beautiful and there's nothing I can do about it*, then walk away. Most people trying to intimidate will be taken aback that they agreed and didn't get upset, and will probably leave them alone thereafter. They can wish their critics well in the challenges they are experiencing and get on with their own core business.

It is hard to learn to accept our new bodies, but they are what we have been given, so acceptance is the only option. There is more to a person than just physical appearance, so it is important to focus on that which defines who you actually are. Conversations with a trusted adult or friend can provide support and stability during difficult times.

In the world we live in today the question of sexuality has evolved. It is OK in a teen's voyage of discovery to figure that she may not fit into the traditional norms. She may find out that her friends may not fit there either. At the end of the day your sexuality does not define who you are. Your core business defines who you are as a person. As long as you remember this and can articulate it, you will be OK. Conversations with parents, trusted adults and friends will help you through your doubts and difficulties and keep you focused on your core business.

A teenager may have a permanent physical anomaly, an illness, a learning disability, or some form of special need. There will always be people who like to make comments and sadly their words can be cruel or harsh. Teaching core business by association here is very important. The children have to learn to accept who they are, what their strengths are and how to play to them. If they can do this, people will respect them. If people are cruel, support from a parent, trusted adult or friend, will reinforce their core business and the strengths that they can demonstrate. This will help them identify with their authentic self and they will feel safe and secure in whatever they undertake.

What Is Your Dirty Little Secret?

Every teen has an idea of what he perceives *normal* to be. He believes everyone has a normal family and his is different. He thinks that his parents are embarrassing, that they aren't rich enough, or cool enough. Sometimes these perceptions have some underlying truth. Maybe his mum has depression, his dad is losing his job or they're getting a divorce. It is what it is, but to the teen it's an embarrassment, a social disaster area. As with anything the teenager does not have any control over, the only possible action if confronted or challenged is to shrug and say, *Yes, my dad lost his job and there is nothing I can do about it.* Or, *I KNOW. It is stink, ay? Hopefully he will find another job soon.*

If your teenager at school are being hassled in this way, it is important that they remember and focus on their core business. Their core business is not finding a job for their dad, for example. Their core business is getting an education. No matter what they do, they cannot get their dad a new job. Yes, their dad does not have a job. Knowing and acknowledging this can help to relieve any tension that a teenager may feel. This is another occasion when it is time to have a conversation, initiated by either the parent or the teenager.

Sometimes what is happening in the family of a teenager is actually really sad. There might be a member of the family who has terminal cancer or has died suddenly in a tragic accident or medical event, or there might be a death of a sibling at birth or somewhere in their childhood. The teenager who is only really able to cope with their own goings on may suddenly have to step up to help maintain the functioning of the family, despite having their own sadness and loss to process. Everyone has their own ways to grieve when losing a loved one. A child or teenager does not understand that they can not fix this situation. They are not responsible for the happiness of the parties involved. Anyone needing help with that should not be afraid to ask. It doesn't need to be a secret, and it doesn't have to be tackled alone.

There are occasions when there are high levels of dysfunction within a family. When they occur, it is next to impossible to have a useful conversation or to communicate concern, because the parties involved are unable to properly address the situation. Teens can feel helpless when this happens, but all the same they need to talk to someone. The thought of sharing a secret so deep is mortifying, however, particularly to a teenager, who all too often opts not to and tries to sort it out alone. Many are not mentally equipped to do this, and they need support. They want to avoid confrontation, but really need to be direct and clear to the point. They need to find the strength within themselves to talk to an independent and trusted adult, or a teacher or friend at school. They need to address the problem directly and not talk in hints, so there is no confusion or misinformation. The trusted adult should then acknowledge their concern, and give the necessary support. She will do all they can to remove the teen's sense of responsibility for what is happening. She will remind the teen that the dysfunction does not define them, it is just something they are associated with, but that lies outside their core business.

Sadly, your children can be subject to sexual abuse and there is not necessarily *dysfunction* within their family or friend group. This could happen from an adult they know, who they did trust, a relative, a friend, a date or a stranger. The question is who do they talk to? Where do they go for support? Or do they keep this a secret? The answer is NO, this is not a secret. The answer is they go somewhere, to someone they deeply trust, who can help them. They will help them to address this terrible event, so it does not prevent them from identifying their core business. However, when something terrible like this has been done, the human body and mind will struggle to make sense of it, as it could not control what happened. The person who did this is not well, and sadly your child was a victim of their actions. Their body will do all it can to bury and hide what has happened. You have one serious question to ask your child? *Is this event going to make you or break you?* The choice is theirs. It will be hard, so hard that they have no idea. It could destroy relationships and possibly will, but whoever did this to them needs help and they cannot continue like this either. By talking to a trusted adult or friend not only will they give your child support, but they will remind them of their core business, and that the sexual abuse does not define who they are. This may be a way to prevent depression and anxiety in the very early stages, creating potential happiness so that suicide is not an option for them.

In life we participate in a multitude of activities and events. Some we succeed in, and in others we fail. If we succeed, the success should be celebrated in a gracious manner. Ideally, we should share it, knowing it is something that we have worked hard to achieve. In some cases, it may be luck, but it can still be celebrated. On the other side of the coin, we might fail or bomb out. This can be embarrassing, and our peers may hassle us, but ultimately it teaches us that we need to look at how we can improve. All this means that we have not achieved our core business—*yet*! 'Yet' is a powerful word that inspires learning and perseverance, and offers hope. Accepting failure to reach a goal is hard, but in life it has to be done—one of the alternatives is anxiety and depression.

On a higher level, what if the failure is going to cause trouble, either with parents or the law. This is where the average teen struggles to own the failure, as the consequences are daunting. At the end of the day, however, the teen messed up and should acknowledge that. Such failures seldom happen on purpose, but as the teenage years are learning years some intentions turn out to be beyond the still-developing skill set. When this happens, the teen has got to tell the truth. Lying is not an option. It breeds further lies, which makes the situation a whole lot worse. Parents will be disappointed and will probably growl, but they will certainly get over it and will still love their child. Failure does not redefine core business, or the teen as a person. It was a mistake and one better not repeated. The teen suffers the consequences and moves on.

Parents must acknowledge that, if our children have poor judgement and get into trouble, we have to let them learn the lesson and not cover it up. We have to remember their mistakes do not define their core business. We must also remember that the mistake does not define us as a parent. In the aftermath of a mistake is a great opportunity for a conversation to determine where our children are at. If this is starting to be a pattern then they have not properly identified their core business and need support. Such a discussion might become heated, but that is OK. It is not for parents to fix, we are to support and guide. In this instance, we are supporting and guiding onto a better path.

A Sad Fact

In establishing your core business, you can only ever be responsible for you. You can strive to do well in school, in sports or recreation, in your work, as part of looking after your own personal health and wellbeing. By establishing what is your core business and discarding what is not, you will be doing what you want to do, a sure remedy for depression or anxiety. You are living in the real world, all the choices are yours, you fully support and own them, so in theory you have nothing to worry about.

You cannot be responsible for what other people choose to do. This can be very frustrating in many ways but, try as you may, you can not determine or change other people's destiny. Parents can guide and support their children, help them establish what drives them, and define their core business. If children are struggling, you may need to have an honest and realistic conversation about how things are—in other words, a reality check. This can be hard for parents, for we do not want to see our children hurting, we want to protect them and make everything OK. But we can only show them the path—we cannot tread it for them. Deep down our children know that too.

The reality check can be a hard life lesson. However, if you know your core business and what drives you, the reality check just makes sense as it is a natural progression. That is why it is so important to help and guide your children in defining their core business, and once that is done accepting it as well. If people have ownership of their choices, but also acceptance of what they choose, (particularly from those closest to them) their self worth will multiply.

Many people do not have a strong self worth, and believe they do not deserve to feel good about themselves. This perception may be real or imagined, but nonetheless seems valid to them. This view is particularly prevalent among teens. Without relevant conversations, earlier rather than later, it is hard to change such feelings. The likelihood of depression or anxiety is higher, and things can spiral out of control. The best defence is to have open and honest conversations about whatever is concerning them, to guide them back towards their core business. If a parent is straight up and honest right from the start, calling things as they are, the children will respect this.

In recent years, our children are exposed to more and more major traumatic events. These may be natural disasters like earthquakes, floods, climate change etc or man-made like wars, mass shootings, extreme hate or racist crimes. The media reports these events on a massive scale and on a highly emotive scale to influence their following, and then social media increases the intensity again.

This can be very scary for people, especially teenagers and they are emotionally unable to process the scale of what has happened. They are unable to influence or change what has happened and as a result this can be very unsettling, even producing post traumatic stress like signs and symptoms. All they can focus on is what they can do:

Some examples are:

1. have a safety plan for a natural disaster

2. do their part to help protect our planet from climate change, and hope that others do the same

3. for hate crimes do their part in treating people fairly and with kindness, and hope that others do the same

4. have a safety plan of what they can do if involved or near a mass shooting.

This is when you remind your children of their core business. Your remind them that this event does not define them, and guide and support them to have perspective of what their role is here. In doing so reducing the likelihood of depression and anxiety for our teens.

What happens if parental support and guidance is not enough? What happens if the child is too depressed to cope anymore, and to whom suicide is the final option. What can you do?

This is so hard and so sad, as you cannot fix the problem and you are not responsible for the child's happiness. Your child is responsible for their own happiness. You have to articulate this, to say, *This is not my problem, it is yours, but you will always have my support.* This is a time to get back to the basics—healthy eating, sufficient sleep and exercise, with support from parents, trusted adults and a medical team. There may be tantrums, there may be fights, there may be sulking, that is OK. To ignore the problem and hope it will go away can have tragic consequences. Nationally and internationally the number of suicides has risen to epidemic proportions.

The Consequences of Ignoring Core Business

In consistently engaging with your own core business, you are constantly having a real conversation with yourself about what you actually want to do as well as what you are responsible for. This internal dialogue keeps you honest. It reduces drama, and in every issue you know what to do and it is simple.

For teenagers and young adults, alike, not identifying what their core business is, and continuing to follow a path that is not what they are or want to be, is where people get into trouble. They try to control what they do, but because it is not what they want or believe, they mask it. It is the beginning of self-destructive behaviour, of self–sabotage.

> *Behaviour is said to be **self-sabotaging** when it creates problems and interferes with long-standing goals.*
>
> *The most common **self-sabotaging** behaviours are procrastination, self‑medication with drugs or alcohol, comfort eating, and forms of self injury such as cutting.*
>
> *Self Sabotage,* Psychology Today

To self–sabotage, people interfere with the path or direction they are following. They may still be outwardly successful, but at a cost—to their family, their job, their relationships. And their own well–being. The pattern will repeat and repeat and repeat unless they identify their core business.

To understand this concept can prevent a lot of heartache. If you are not following your core business, you will slowly self destruct. For teenagers, it could be because their parents are continuously on their case to complete basic tasks, shine at school, excel at sporting activities or performing arts. Their destructive behaviour increases, as what they are doing or contemplating is not what they truly desire. They might start hanging out with friends who are a bad influence, they might start drinking a lot or doing drugs. Their study, activities or work start going downhill. Parents need to probe and discuss until they can break down what your teenager is wanting to do, help them define their authentic self. There will be battles, but parents should keep probing and keep trying till they guide the teenager into a pathway that she is happy with.

The classic response from a teenager asked, *What do you want to do when you leave school?* is a simple, *I'm not sure.* It is as though by not answering she cannot give you the wrong answer. But there is no wrong answer. Whatever your teenager decides to do with her life, as she approaches adulthood she will become perfectly capable of picking what is right for her. The decision is hers, and it actually doesn't actually matter what she chooses. Advice or suggestions from parents and teachers are OK, but she is responsible for weighing up the pros and cons, and can decide what is best for them. If you are following your core business or what is right for you, with absolute ownership here, self sabotage will never even enter the picture.

If you are engaged in activities that you are truly passionate about, self–sabotage is not an option.

To forestall self-sabotage, you need to realise that the behaviour is destructive.; You ask yourself, *What is my core business here?* If you find yourself being drawn to this behaviour, ask yourself, *What am I masking?* The answer might not seem obvious at first, but by looking at all aspects of your life you can figure it out.

Addiction to social media and electronic devices can be a consequence of not pursuing your core business. Many devices affect the brain as if the user was taking drugs. It is tempting to portray via social media a persona that is happy, and handsome and successful. The image is not real, and rarely relates to core business. It portrays a person that society may admire, but if it does not align with your core business, no matter how many 'likes' you score, you will be left unsatisfied. You are responsible for your own happiness, and no one else. Happiness is not determined by recognition in social media.

Obsessive gaming can be another sign of self sabotage, and denial of core business. If gaming is not intelligently managed, people can lose any sense of who they are and where they're going. They are lost in a fantasy world in which there are no consequences for unlawful behaviour, a perception that can carry over into real life and be echoed in antisocial activity.

By knowing and engaging in your core business, you can limit the use of electronic devices to what they're designed to be—a vehicle for entertainment, connection and relaxation. Electronic entertainment is part of the world we live in. Treated respectfully it has a lot of added value need not be self sabotaging at all. The main point is to set your boundaries to keep it safe, effective and real.

Another consequence of not committing to your core business is anger and frustration, and unhappiness. This can be very obvious at the end of the day, when tired teenagers or adults are ill–tempered and snappy. If proper food, sleep and hydration have been provided the irritability may simply indicate that someone hasn't been pursuing core business. Loved ones may get very intolerant as they see only bad behaviour. They need to understand that the bad behaviour does not reflect on them, but is a sign that the grumpy one needs help with his core business.

There can be a serious impact on your health, either physically or on your own mental health, as another consequence. Your body and mind know that you have not addressed your core business and it is doing what it knows best to survive. This may be through anxiety, depression or even further complex mental illness. The hard part about identifying your core business is there may be consequences to you, your family or friends and how that could unfold is frightening. The truth is it is frightening. It is almost easier to not face it, but this prevents you from becoming a true version of who you are meant to be. In your body's protection of yourself, you become unwell and 'labelled' for not coping. The minute you allow yourself to follow your true core business, after the fallout has settled, or maybe there wasn't even any fallout as it was all perceived, your brain will relax and you will feel better.

Finally ...

About seven years ago, I saw the You Tube clip, *BOATLIFT–An Untold Tale of 9/11 Resilience*. To give you some background, when 9/11 unfolded there was no way to get the people trapped in Manhattan off the island. A call was put out to boat owners asking for their help. Boats of all shapes and sizes converged on Manhattan Island and in less than nine hours nearly 500,000 people were evacuated. One of the boat owners said some things that resonated with me, notably:

"If I save one person that will be one less person to suffer and die"

"I have one theory in life, I never want to say 'I should have ... 'If I do it and fail, I tried. If I do it and succeed then better for me. Never go through life saying 'I should have.' If you want to do it, do it!"

On my birthday, the 4th of July, I found my boat lift. Too many young people are dying and too many seem to follow a similar pattern, as I have had the same conversations repeatedly over the years with people who have come through my clinic. Something has got to be done. I want to change basic perspective and create a paradigm shift in thinking. I believe that identifying and engaging in what is real and important—core business— is the way to go. I want to get this idea out there to help our youth find direction and stability, and reach maturity successfully.

Acknowledgements

My children Ben and Robbie for having this project as a constant source of conversation in our household. Thank you for your patience.

The people through the years at work or in my community, that through conversations, or provided clinical experience that has planted the source of ideas to make this book comprehensive for this topic of suicide prevention.

My parents for teaching me straight up common sense, so that these ideas are just the way it is.